Skipper Kipper
and the Treasure Chest

Written by
Jill Atkins

Illustrated by
Andy Hamilton

Ransom

Skipper Kipper jumped onto the deck of his ship, the Daft Dog.

"Crew!" he hollered. "We are going on a treasure hunt!"

"Hooray!" shouted Cabin Boy Alf. "Treasure hunts are fantastic fun!"

"I agree," called Best Mate Lily. "Count me in!"

3

Skipper Kipper stood at the ship's wheel and away they went, sailing across the sparkling sea.

They sped through the waves, until suddenly …

"Caw! Caw!"

Kipper looked up. Claw, the scarlet macaw, was perched high on the crow's nest. She was pointing into the distance.

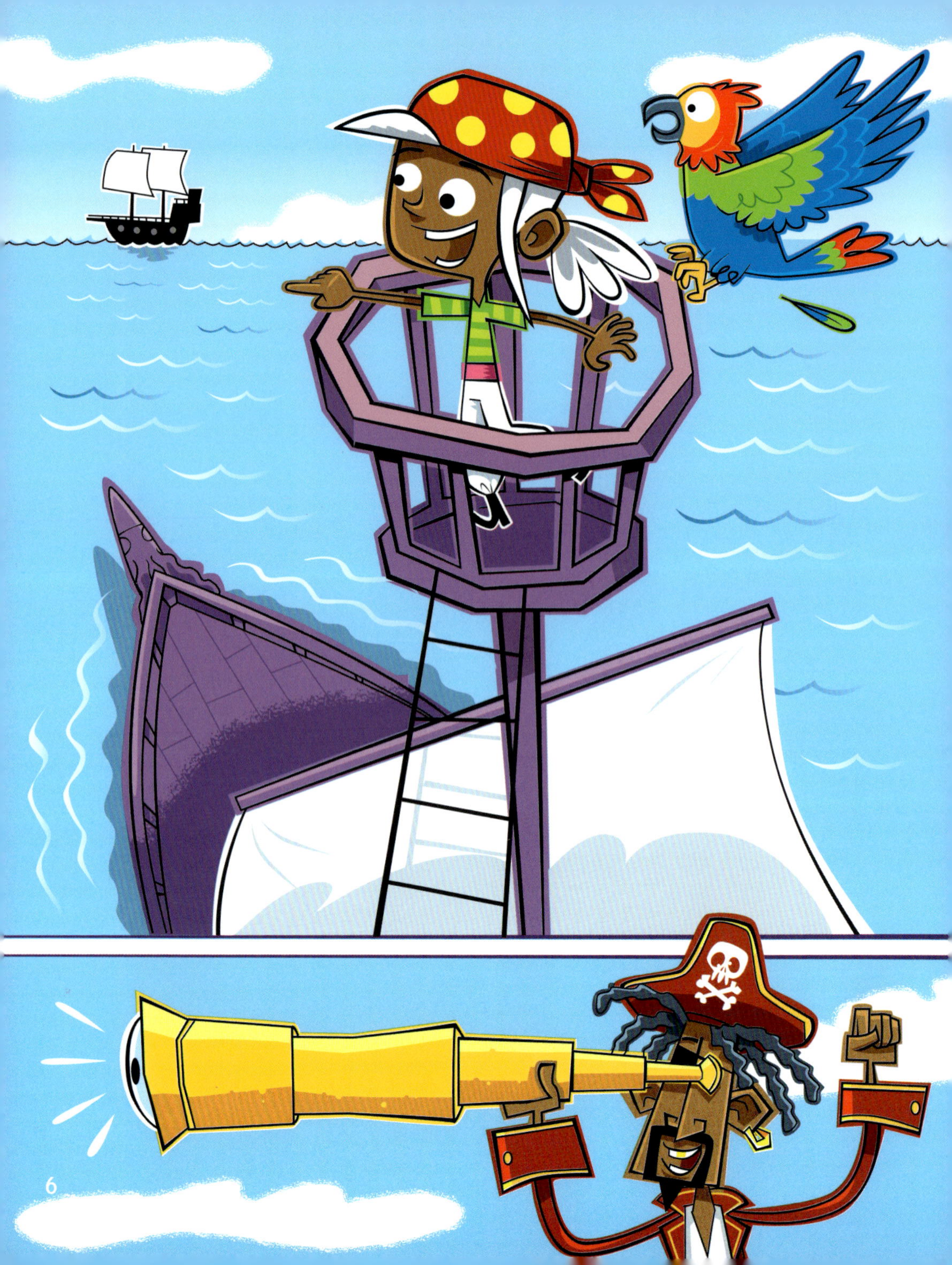

Lily quickly nipped up the rigging to join her.

"Yes!" Lily called. "There **is** a ship. Let us chase it."

Kipper looked at the ship through his telescope.

"It's the Flying Frog!" he shouted. "I bet they have some treasure."

Soon they reached the Flying Frog.

"There **is** a treasure chest on the deck," called Lily.

"Hooray!" shouted Alf.

"Get the Magic Masher out!" called Kipper.

Alf dragged out the catapult.

"Fire!" yelled Kipper.

Lumps of mashed potato flew through the air and landed on the crew of the Flying Frog.

In swooped Claw Macaw. She grabbed the chest in her claws and flew back to the Daft Dog.

Skipper Kipper turned the wheel and off they went.

After a while, Alf sniffed.

"What is that pong?" he asked.

They looked at the treasure chest.

"I think it is coming from there," said Lily. She lifted the lid.

"Phew!" she cried. "What a pong!"

11

Alf peered into the chest.

"Oh no!" he yelled.

"What is it?" asked Kipper.

"It's … cheese!" cried Lily, faintly.

"Cheese?" Skipper Kipper nearly exploded. "No treasure?"

Alf and Lily shook their heads.

"Don't worry. Just shut the lid, please!" cried Kipper. "We will have to take it back to the Flying Frog."

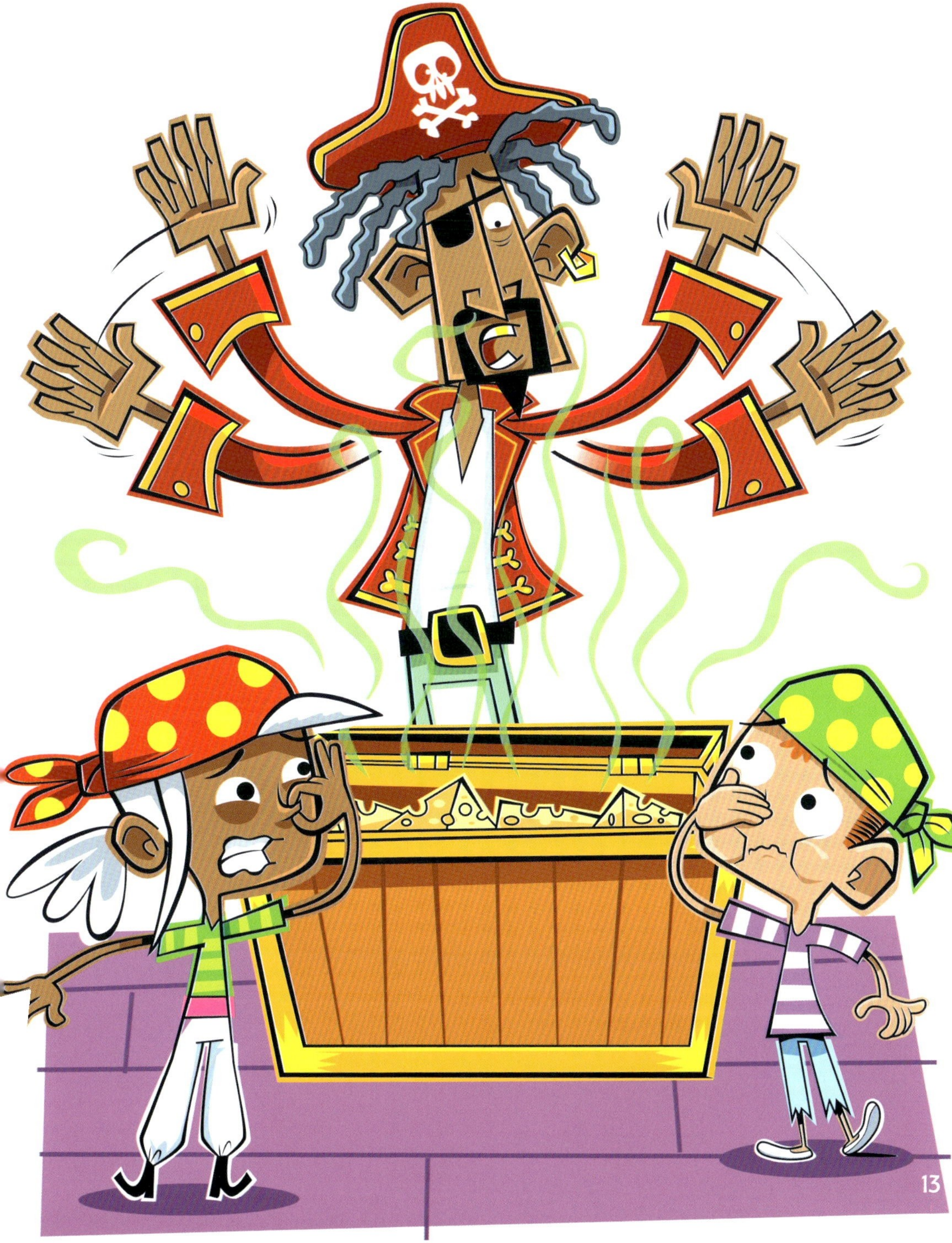

Quickly, they headed back to the Flying Frog.

"Get the Splatter Gun!" ordered the skipper.

Alf pulled out the gun.

"Fire!" yelled Kipper.

Red paint flew from the Splatter Gun onto the crew of the Flying Frog.

Claw lifted the chest. She swooped across to the Flying Frog and dropped the chest onto the deck.

Then they made their escape.

"Phew!" said Lily. "What shall we do now?"

"Well," said Kipper. "We set off to find treasure …

so that is exactly what we will do!"

"Hooray!" shouted Alf. "I love treasure hunts."

"So *please*, let it be real treasure this time!" laughed Lily.